THE SWIMMERS
Journal

Name _____

Age _____

Year _____

Swim Club

Training Days

MON **TUES** **WED** **THURS** **FRI**

SAT **SUN**

©The Life Graduate Publishing Group

No part of this book may be scanned, reproduced or distributed in any printed or electronic form without the prior permission of the author or publisher.

01

SWIMMING GOALS

01
6 MONTH TRAINING GOALS

GOAL 1
....
....
....

GOAL 2
....
....
....

GOAL 3
....
....
....

GOAL 4
....
....
....

SWIM MEET GOALS

GOAL 1
....
....
....

GOAL 2
....
....
....

GOAL 3
....
....
....

"For myself, losing is not coming second. It's getting out of the water knowing you could have done better. For myslef, I have won every race I've been in"

-Ian Thorpe-

02

TRAINING LOGBOOK

TRAINING SESSION LOGBOOK

Date: / /

Start time :

End time :

Total Training Time   HRS   MINS

Total Distance Swam

Location ....

Details of the Session

Warm-Up

....
....
....
....

Main Set

....
....
....
....
....

Cool Down

....
....
....

Additional Notes/Information Coach feedback? Swimming partner details? Areas to work on for next session?

....
....
....

TRAINING SESSION LOGBOOK

Date: / /

Start time :

End time :

Total Training Time HRS MINS

Total Distance Swam

Location ....

Details of the Session

Warm-Up

....
....
....
....

Main Set

....
....
....
....
....

Cool Down

....
....
....

Additional Notes/Information Coach feedback? Swimming partner details? Areas to work on for next session?

....
....
....

TRAINING SESSION LOGBOOK

Date: /   /   **Start time**   :

                                                             End time   :

Total Training Time   HRS   MINS

Total Distance Swam

Location ....

Details of the Session

Warm-Up

....
....
....
....

Main Set

....
....
....
....
....
....

Cool Down

....
....
....

Additional Notes/Information Coach feedback? Swimming partner details? Areas to work on for next session?

....
....
....

TRAINING SESSION LOGBOOK

Date: /   /   **Start time**   :

                              End time   :

Total Training Time   HRS   MINS

Total Distance Swam

Location ....

Details of the Session

Warm-Up

....
....
....
....

Main Set

....
....
....
....
....
....

Cool Down

....
....
....

Additional Notes/Information Coach feedback? Swimming partner details? Areas to work on for next session?

....
....
....

TRAINING SESSION LOGBOOK

Date: /   /   **Start time**   :

                             End time   :

Total Training Time   HRS   MINS

Total Distance Swam

Location ....

Details of the Session

Warm-Up

....
....
....
....

Main Set

....
....
....
....
....

Cool Down

....
....
....

Additional Notes/Information Coach feedback? Swimming partner details? Areas to work on for next session?

....
....
....

TRAINING SESSION LOGBOOK

Date: / /   **Start time** :

End time :

Total Training Time   HRS   MINS

Total Distance Swam

Location ....

Details of the Session

Warm-Up

....
....
....
....

Main Set

....
....
....
....
....

Cool Down

....
....
....

Additional Notes/Information Coach feedback? Swimming partner details? Areas to work on for next session?

....
....
....

TRAINING SESSION LOGBOOK

Date: /   /

Start time   :

End time   :

Total Training Time   HRS   MINS

Total Distance Swam

Location ....

Details of the Session

Warm-Up

....
....
....
....

Main Set

....
....
....
....
....
....

Cool Down

....
....
....

Additional Notes/Information Coach feedback? Swimming partner details? Areas to work on for next session?

....
....
....

7 SESSION REFLECTION

Date: /   /

Total training time for past 7 sessions: HRS   MINS

Total distance of swimming for past 7 sessions:

Overall, my training sessions for the past 7 days have been:

Excellent   Very Good   Good   Poor

Feedback/Notes From Swim Sessions

....
....
....
....

Other Details   How are you feeling? Is your training progressing as planned? Have you specific goals you wish to achieve for your next 7 training sessions?

....
....
....
....
....
....
....
....

TRAINING SESSION LOGBOOK

Date: /   /   **Start time**   :

End time   :

Total Training Time   HRS   MINS

Total Distance Swam

Location ....

Details of the Session

Warm-Up

....
....
....
....

Main Set

....
....
....
....
....
....

Cool Down

....
....
....

Additional Notes/Information Coach feedback? Swimming partner details? Areas to work on for next session?

....
....
....

TRAINING SESSION LOGBOOK

Date: /   /   **Start time**   :

End time   :

Total Training Time   HRS   MINS

Total Distance Swam

Location ....

Details of the Session

Warm-Up

....
....
....
....

Main Set

....
....
....
....
....
....

Cool Down

....
....
....

Additional Notes/Information Coach feedback? Swimming partner details? Areas to work on for next session?

....
....
....

TRAINING SESSION LOGBOOK

Date: /   /   **Start time**   :

                                           End time   :

Total Training Time   HRS   MINS

Total Distance Swam

Location ....

Details of the Session

Warm-Up

....

....

....

....

Main Set

....

....

....

....

....

....

Cool Down

....

....

....

Additional Notes/Information Coach feedback? Swimming partner details? Areas to work on for next session?

....

....

....

TRAINING SESSION LOGBOOK

Date: / /

Start time :

End time :

Total Training Time   HRS   MINS

Total Distance Swam

Location ....

Details of the Session

Warm-Up

....
....
....
....

Main Set

....
....
....
....
....

Cool Down

....
....
....

Additional Notes/Information
Coach feedback? Swimming partner details? Areas to work on for next session?

....
....
....

TRAINING SESSION LOGBOOK

Date: / / **Start time** :

 End time :

Total Training Time   HRS   MINS

Total Distance Swam

Location ....

Details of the Session

Warm-Up

....
....
....
....

Main Set

....
....
....
....
....

Cool Down

....
....
....

Additional Notes/Information Coach feedback? Swimming partner details? Areas to work on for next session?

....
....
....

TRAINING SESSION LOGBOOK

Date: /   /   **Start time**   :

                              End time   :

Total Training Time   HRS   MINS

Total Distance Swam

Location ....

Details of the Session

Warm-Up

....
....
....
....

Main Set

....
....
....
....
....

Cool Down

....
....
....

Additional Notes/Information   Coach feedback? Swimming partner details? Areas to work on for next session?

....
....
....

TRAINING SESSION LOGBOOK

Date: / /   **Start time** :

End time :

Total Training Time   HRS   MINS

Total Distance Swam

Location ....

Details of the Session

Warm-Up

....
....
....
....

Main Set

....
....
....
....
....

Cool Down

....
....
....

Additional Notes/Information Coach feedback? Swimming partner details? Areas to work on for next session?

....
....
....

7 SESSION REFLECTION

Date: /   /

Total training time for past 7 sessions: HRS   MINS

Total distance of swimming for past 7 sessions:

Overall, my training sessions for the past 7 days have been:

Excellent   Very Good   Good   Poor

Feedback/Notes From Swim Sessions

....
....
....
....

Other Details   How are you feeling? Is your training progressing as planned? Have you specific goals you wish to achieve for your next 7 training sessions?

....
....
....
....
....
....
....
....

TRAINING SESSION LOGBOOK

Date: /   /   **Start time**   :

End time   :

Total Training Time   HRS   MINS

Total Distance Swam

Location ....

Details of the Session

Warm-Up

....
....
....
....

Main Set

....
....
....
....
....

Cool Down

....
....
....

Additional Notes/Information Coach feedback? Swimming partner details? Areas to work on for next session?

....
....
....

TRAINING SESSION LOGBOOK

Date: / /   **Start time** :

End time :

Total Training Time   HRS   MINS

Total Distance Swam

Location ....

Details of the Session

Warm-Up

....
....
....
....

Main Set

....
....
....
....
....

Cool Down

....
....
....

Additional Notes/Information Coach feedback? Swimming partner details? Areas to work on for next session?

....
....
....

TRAINING SESSION LOGBOOK

Date: /   /   **Start time**   :

End time   :

Total Training Time   HRS   MINS

Total Distance Swam

Location ....

Details of the Session

Warm-Up

....
....
....
....

Main Set

....
....
....
....
....
....

Cool Down

....
....
....

Additional Notes/Information Coach feedback? Swimming partner details? Areas to work on for next session?

....
....
....

TRAINING SESSION LOGBOOK

Date: / / **Start time** :

End time :

Total Training Time   HRS   MINS

Total Distance Swam

Location ....

Details of the Session

Warm-Up

....
....
....
....

Main Set

....
....
....
....
....

Cool Down

....
....
....

Additional Notes/Information Coach feedback? Swimming partner details? Areas to work on for next session?

....
....
....

TRAINING SESSION LOGBOOK

Date: /   /   **Start time**   :

End time   :

Total Training Time   HRS   MINS

Total Distance Swam

Location ....

Details of the Session

Warm-Up

....
....
....
....

Main Set

....
....
....
....
....

Cool Down

....
....
....

Additional Notes/Information   Coach feedback? Swimming partner details? Areas to work on for next session?

....
....
....

TRAINING SESSION LOGBOOK

Date: / /

Start time :

End time :

Total Training Time   HRS   MINS

Total Distance Swam

Location ....

Details of the Session

Warm-Up

....
....
....
....

Main Set

....
....
....
....
....

Cool Down

....
....
....

Additional Notes/Information Coach feedback? Swimming partner details? Areas to work on for next session?

....
....
....

TRAINING SESSION LOGBOOK

Date: /   /   **Start time**   :

End time   :

Total Training Time   HRS   MINS

Total Distance Swam

Location ....

Details of the Session

Warm-Up

....
....
....
....

Main Set

....
....
....
....
....

Cool Down

....
....
....

Additional Notes/Information   Coach feedback? Swimming partner details? Areas to work on for next session?

....
....
....

7 SESSION REFLECTION

Date: / /

Total training time for past 7 sessions: HRS   MINS

Total distance of swimming for past 7 sessions:

Overall, my training sessions for the past 7 days have been:

Excellent   Very Good   Good   Poor

Feedback/Notes From Swim Sessions

....
....
....
....

Other Details — How are you feeling? Is your training progressing as planned? Have you specific goals you wish to achieve for your next 7 training sessions?

....
....
....
....
....
....
....
....

TRAINING SESSION LOGBOOK

Date: / /

Start time :

End time :

Total Training Time   HRS   MINS

Total Distance Swam

Location ....

Details of the Session

Warm-Up

....
....
....
....

Main Set

....
....
....
....
....

Cool Down

....
....
....

Additional Notes/Information Coach feedback? Swimming partner details? Areas to work on for next session?

....
....
....

TRAINING SESSION LOGBOOK

Date: / /

Start time :

End time :

Total Training Time   HRS   MINS

Total Distance Swam

Location ....

Details of the Session

Warm-Up

....
....
....
....

Main Set

....
....
....
....
....

Cool Down

....
....
....

Additional Notes/Information Coach feedback? Swimming partner details? Areas to work on for next session?

....
....
....

TRAINING SESSION LOGBOOK

Date: /   /

Start time   :

End time   :

Total Training Time   HRS   MINS

Total Distance Swam

Location ....

Details of the Session

Warm-Up

....
....
....
....

Main Set

....
....
....
....
....

Cool Down

....
....
....

Additional Notes/Information Coach feedback? Swimming partner details? Areas to work on for next session?

....
....
....

TRAINING SESSION LOGBOOK

Date: /   /   **Start time**   :

End time   :

Total Training Time   HRS   MINS

Total Distance Swam

Location ....

Details of the Session

Warm-Up

....
....
....
....

Main Set

....
....
....
....
....

Cool Down

....
....
....

Additional Notes/Information Coach feedback? Swimming partner details? Areas to work on for next session?

....
....
....

TRAINING SESSION LOGBOOK

Date: / /   **Start time** :

End time :

Total Training Time   HRS   MINS

Total Distance Swam

Location ....

Details of the Session

Warm-Up

....
....
....
....

Main Set

....
....
....
....
....

Cool Down

....
....
....

Additional Notes/Information Coach feedback? Swimming partner details? Areas to work on for next session?

....
....
....

TRAINING SESSION LOGBOOK

Date: / /   **Start time** :

End time :

Total Training Time   HRS   MINS

Total Distance Swam

Location ....

Details of the Session

Warm-Up

....
....
....
....

Main Set

....
....
....
....
....

Cool Down

....
....
....

Additional Notes/Information Coach feedback? Swimming partner details? Areas to work on for next session?

....
....
....

TRAINING SESSION LOGBOOK

Date: / /   **Start time** :

End time :

Total Training Time   HRS   MINS

Total Distance Swam

Location ....

Details of the Session

Warm-Up

....
....
....
....

Main Set

....
....
....
....
....
....

Cool Down

....
....
....

Additional Notes/Information Coach feedback? Swimming partner details? Areas to work on for next session?

....
....
....

7 SESSION REFLECTION

Date: /   /

Total training time for past 7 sessions: HRS   MINS

Total distance of swimming for past 7 sessions:

Overall, my training sessions for the past 7 days have been:

Excellent   Very Good   Good   Poor

Feedback/Notes From Swim Sessions

....
....
....
....

Other Details — How are you feeling? Is your training progressing as planned? Have you specific goals you wish to achieve for your next 7 training sessions?

....
....
....
....
....
....
....
....
....

TRAINING SESSION LOGBOOK

Date: / /

Start time :

End time :

Total Training Time   HRS   MINS

Total Distance Swam

Location ....

Details of the Session

Warm-Up

....
....
....
....

Main Set

....
....
....
....
....

Cool Down

....
....
....

Additional Notes/Information Coach feedback? Swimming partner details? Areas to work on for next session?

....
....
....

TRAINING SESSION LOGBOOK

Date: / /   **Start time** :

End time :

Total Training Time   HRS   MINS

Total Distance Swam

Location ....

Details of the Session

Warm-Up

....
....
....
....

Main Set

....
....
....
....
....

Cool Down

....
....
....

Additional Notes/Information   Coach feedback? Swimming partner details? Areas to work on for next session?

....
....
....

TRAINING SESSION LOGBOOK

Date: / /   **Start time** :

End time :

Total Training Time   HRS   MINS

Total Distance Swam

Location ....

Details of the Session

Warm-Up

....

....

....

....

Main Set

....

....

....

....

....

Cool Down

....

....

....

Additional Notes/Information Coach feedback? Swimming partner details? Areas to work on for next session?

....

....

....

TRAINING SESSION LOGBOOK

Date: /   /   **Start time**   :

                                      End time   :

Total Training Time   HRS   MINS

Total Distance Swam

Location ....

Details of the Session

Warm-Up

....
....
....
....

Main Set

....
....
....
....
....

Cool Down

....
....
....

Additional Notes/Information Coach feedback? Swimming partner details? Areas to work on for next session?

....
....
....

TRAINING SESSION LOGBOOK

Date: / /

Start time :

End time :

Total Training Time   HRS   MINS

Total Distance Swam

Location ....

Details of the Session

Warm-Up

....
....
....
....

Main Set

....
....
....
....
....

Cool Down

....
....
....

Additional Notes/Information Coach feedback? Swimming partner details? Areas to work on for next session?

....
....
....

TRAINING SESSION LOGBOOK

Date: / /   **Start time** :

End time :

Total Training Time   HRS   MINS

Total Distance Swam

Location ....

Details of the Session

Warm-Up

....
....
....
....

Main Set

....
....
....
....
....

Cool Down

....
....
....

Additional Notes/Information Coach feedback? Swimming partner details? Areas to work on for next session?

....
....
....

TRAINING SESSION LOGBOOK

Date: / / **Start time** :

End time :

Total Training Time   HRS   MINS

Total Distance Swam

Location ....

Details of the Session

Warm-Up

....
....
....
....

Main Set

....
....
....
....
....
....

Cool Down

....
....
....

Additional Notes/Information Coach feedback? Swimming partner details? Areas to work on for next session?

....
....
....

7 SESSION REFLECTION

Date: /   /

Total training time for past 7 sessions: HRS   MINS

Total distance of swimming for past 7 sessions:

Overall, my training sessions for the past 7 days have been:

Excellent   Very Good   Good   Poor

Feedback/Notes From Swim Sessions

....
....
....
....

Other Details — How are you feeling? Is your training progressing as planned? Have you specific goals you wish to achieve for your next 7 training sessions?

....
....
....
....
....
....
....
....

TRAINING SESSION LOGBOOK

Date: / /   **Start time** :

End time :

Total Training Time   HRS   MINS

Total Distance Swam

Location ....

Details of the Session

Warm-Up

....
....
....
....

Main Set

....
....
....
....
....

Cool Down

....
....
....

Additional Notes/Information Coach feedback? Swimming partner details? Areas to work on for next session?

....
....
....

TRAINING SESSION LOGBOOK

Date: /   /   **Start time**   :

End time   :

Total Training Time   HRS   MINS

Total Distance Swam

Location ....

Details of the Session

Warm-Up

....
....
....
....

Main Set

....
....
....
....
....

Cool Down

....
....
....

Additional Notes/Information Coach feedback? Swimming partner details? Areas to work on for next session?

....
....
....

TRAINING SESSION LOGBOOK

Date: /   /   **Start time**   :

                                            End time   :

Total Training Time   HRS   MINS

Total Distance Swam

Location ....

Details of the Session

Warm-Up

....
....
....
....

Main Set

....
....
....
....
....
....

Cool Down

....
....
....

Additional Notes/Information Coach feedback? Swimming partner details? Areas to work on for next session?

....
....
....

TRAINING SESSION LOGBOOK

Date: / /

Start time :

End time :

Total Training Time   HRS   MINS

Total Distance Swam

Location ....

Details of the Session

Warm-Up

....
....
....
....

Main Set

....
....
....
....
....

Cool Down

....
....
....

Additional Notes/Information Coach feedback? Swimming partner details? Areas to work on for next session?

....
....
....

TRAINING SESSION LOGBOOK

Date:　　/　　/　　　　**Start time**　　:

　　　　　　　　　　　　　End time　　　:

Total Training Time　　　HRS　　　MINS

Total Distance Swam

Location ....

Details of the Session

Warm-Up

....
....
....
....

Main Set

....
....
....
....
....
....

Cool Down

....
....
....

Additional Notes/Information Coach feedback? Swimming partner details? Areas to work on for next session?

....
....
....

TRAINING SESSION LOGBOOK

Date: /   /   **Start time**   :

                               End time   :

Total Training Time   HRS   MINS

Total Distance Swam

Location ....

Details of the Session

Warm-Up

....
....
....
....

Main Set

....
....
....
....
....
....

Cool Down

....
....
....

Additional Notes/Information Coach feedback? Swimming partner details? Areas to work on for next session?

....
....
....

TRAINING SESSION LOGBOOK

Date: /   /   **Start time**   :

                              End time   :

Total Training Time   HRS   MINS

Total Distance Swam

Location ....

Details of the Session

Warm-Up

....
....
....
....

Main Set

....
....
....
....
....

Cool Down

....
....
....

Additional Notes/Information Coach feedback? Swimming partner details? Areas to work on for next session?

....
....
....

7 SESSION REFLECTION

Date: /   /

Total training time for past 7 sessions: HRS   MINS

Total distance of swimming for past 7 sessions:

Overall, my training sessions for the past 7 days have been:

Excellent   Very Good   Good   Poor

Feedback/Notes From Swim Sessions

....
....
....
....

Other Details   How are you feeling? Is your training progressing as planned? Have you specific goals you wish to achieve for your next 7 training sessions?

....
....
....
....
....
....
....
....

TRAINING SESSION LOGBOOK

Date: / /   **Start time** :

End time :

Total Training Time   HRS   MINS

Total Distance Swam

Location ....

Details of the Session

Warm-Up

....
....
....
....

Main Set

....
....
....
....
....
....

Cool Down

....
....
....

Additional Notes/Information Coach feedback? Swimming partner details? Areas to work on for next session?

....
....
....

TRAINING SESSION LOGBOOK

Date: / /   **Start time** :

End time :

Total Training Time HRS MINS

Total Distance Swam

Location ....

Details of the Session

Warm-Up

....
....
....
....

Main Set

....
....
....
....
....

Cool Down

....
....
....

Additional Notes/Information Coach feedback? Swimming partner details? Areas to work on for next session?

....
....
....

TRAINING SESSION LOGBOOK

Date: /   /   **Start time**   :

End time   :

Total Training Time   HRS   MINS

Total Distance Swam

Location ....

Details of the Session

Warm-Up

....
....
....
....

Main Set

....
....
....
....
....

Cool Down

....
....
....

Additional Notes/Information Coach feedback? Swimming partner details? Areas to work on for next session?

....
....
....

TRAINING SESSION LOGBOOK

Date: / /

Start time :

End time :

Total Training Time　　　HRS　　　MINS

Total Distance Swam

Location ....

Details of the Session

Warm-Up

....
....
....
....

Main Set

....
....
....
....
....

Cool Down

....
....
....

Additional Notes/Information Coach feedback? Swimming partner details? Areas to work on for next session?

....
....
....

TRAINING SESSION LOGBOOK

Date: / /

Start time :

End time :

Total Training Time   HRS   MINS

Total Distance Swam

Location ....

Details of the Session

Warm-Up

....
....
....
....

Main Set

....
....
....
....
....
....

Cool Down

....
....
....

Additional Notes/Information Coach feedback? Swimming partner details? Areas to work on for next session?

....
....
....

TRAINING SESSION LOGBOOK

Date: / /   **Start time** :

End time :

Total Training Time   HRS   MINS

Total Distance Swam

Location ....

Details of the Session

Warm-Up

....
....
....
....

Main Set

....
....
....
....
....

Cool Down

....
....
....

Additional Notes/Information Coach feedback? Swimming partner details? Areas to work on for next session?

....
....
....

TRAINING SESSION LOGBOOK

Date: /   /   **Start time**   :

                                   End time   :

Total Training Time   HRS   MINS

Total Distance Swam

Location ....

Details of the Session

Warm-Up

....

....

....

....

Main Set

....

....

....

....

....

Cool Down

....

....

....

Additional Notes/Information Coach feedback? Swimming partner details? Areas to work on for next session?

....

....

....

7 SESSION REFLECTION

Date: / /

Total training time for past 7 sessions: HRS MINS

Total distance of swimming for past 7 sessions:

Overall, my training sessions for the past 7 days have been:

Excellent   Very Good   Good   Poor

Feedback/Notes From Swim Sessions

....
....
....
....

Other Details   How are you feeling? Is your training progressing as planned? Have you specific goals you wish to achieve for your next 7 training sessions?

....
....
....
....
....
....
....
....

TRAINING SESSION LOGBOOK

Date: /   /   **Start time**   :

                              End time   :

Total Training Time   HRS   MINS

Total Distance Swam

Location ....

Details of the Session

Warm-Up

....
....
....
....

Main Set

....
....
....
....
....

Cool Down

....
....
....

Additional Notes/Information Coach feedback? Swimming partner details? Areas to work on for next session?

....
....
....

TRAINING SESSION LOGBOOK

Date: / /   **Start time** :

End time :

Total Training Time   HRS   MINS

Total Distance Swam

Location ....

Details of the Session

Warm-Up

....
....
....
....

Main Set

....
....
....
....
....

Cool Down

....
....
....

Additional Notes/Information Coach feedback? Swimming partner details? Areas to work on for next session?

....
....
....

TRAINING SESSION LOGBOOK

Date: /   /   **Start time**   :

End time   :

Total Training Time   HRS   MINS

Total Distance Swam

Location ....

Details of the Session

Warm-Up

....
....
....
....

Main Set

....
....
....
....
....
....

Cool Down

....
....
....

Additional Notes/Information   Coach feedback? Swimming partner details? Areas to work on for next session?

....
....
....

TRAINING SESSION LOGBOOK

Date: / /

Start time :

End time :

Total Training Time   HRS   MINS

Total Distance Swam

Location ....

Details of the Session

Warm-Up

....
....
....
....

Main Set

....
....
....
....
....

Cool Down

....
....
....

Additional Notes/Information Coach feedback? Swimming partner details? Areas to work on for next session?

....
....
....

TRAINING SESSION LOGBOOK

Date: / / **Start time** :

End time :

Total Training Time   HRS   MINS

Total Distance Swam

Location ....

Details of the Session

Warm-Up

....
....
....
....

Main Set

....
....
....
....
....

Cool Down

....
....
....

Additional Notes/Information Coach feedback? Swimming partner details? Areas to work on for next session?

....
....
....

TRAINING SESSION LOGBOOK

Date: / /   **Start time** :

                        End time :

Total Training Time   HRS   MINS

Total Distance Swam

Location ....

Details of the Session

Warm-Up

....
....
....
....

Main Set

....
....
....
....
....
....

Cool Down

....
....
....

Additional Notes/Information Coach feedback? Swimming partner details? Areas to work on for next session?

....
....
....

TRAINING SESSION LOGBOOK

Date: /   /   **Start time**   :

End time   :

Total Training Time   HRS   MINS

Total Distance Swam

Location ....

Details of the Session

Warm-Up

....
....
....
....

Main Set

....
....
....
....
....
....

Cool Down

....
....
....

Additional Notes/Information Coach feedback? Swimming partner details? Areas to work on for next session?

....
....
....

7 SESSION REFLECTION

Date: /   /

Total training time for past 7 sessions: HRS   MINS

Total distance of swimming for past 7 sessions:

Overall, my training sessions for the past 7 days have been:

Excellent   Very Good   Good   Poor

Feedback/Notes From Swim Sessions

....
....
....
....

Other Details — How are you feeling? Is your training progressing as planned? Have you specific goals you wish to achieve for your next 7 training sessions?

....
....
....
....
....
....
....
....

TRAINING SESSION LOGBOOK

Date: / /   **Start time** :

End time :

Total Training Time   HRS   MINS

Total Distance Swam

Location ....

Details of the Session

Warm-Up

....
....
....
....

Main Set

....
....
....
....
....

Cool Down

....
....
....

Additional Notes/Information Coach feedback? Swimming partner details? Areas to work on for next session?

....
....
....

TRAINING SESSION LOGBOOK

Date: /   /   **Start time**   :

                                             End time   :

Total Training Time   HRS   MINS

Total Distance Swam

Location ....

Details of the Session

Warm-Up

....
....
....
....

Main Set

....
....
....
....
....

Cool Down

....
....
....

Additional Notes/Information Coach feedback? Swimming partner details? Areas to work on for next session?

....
....
....

TRAINING SESSION LOGBOOK

Date: / /   **Start time** :

End time :

Total Training Time   HRS   MINS

Total Distance Swam

Location ....

Details of the Session

Warm-Up

....
....
....
....

Main Set

....
....
....
....
....

Cool Down

....
....
....

Additional Notes/Information Coach feedback? Swimming partner details? Areas to work on for next session?

....
....
....

TRAINING SESSION LOGBOOK

Date: /   /

Start time   :

End time   :

Total Training Time   HRS   MINS

Total Distance Swam

Location ....

Details of the Session

Warm-Up

....
....
....
....

Main Set

....
....
....
....
....

Cool Down

....
....
....

Additional Notes/Information Coach feedback? Swimming partner details? Areas to work on for next session?

....
....
....

TRAINING SESSION LOGBOOK

Date: /   /   **Start time**   :

End time   :

Total Training Time   HRS   MINS

Total Distance Swam

Location ....

Details of the Session

Warm-Up

....
....
....
....

Main Set

....
....
....
....
....

Cool Down

....
....
....

Additional Notes/Information Coach feedback? Swimming partner details? Areas to work on for next session?

....
....
....

TRAINING SESSION LOGBOOK

Date: / /

Start time :

End time :

Total Training Time   HRS   MINS

Total Distance Swam

Location ....

Details of the Session

Warm-Up

....
....
....
....

Main Set

....
....
....
....
....

Cool Down

....
....
....

Additional Notes/Information Coach feedback? Swimming partner details? Areas to work on for next session?

....
....
....

TRAINING SESSION LOGBOOK

Date: /   /   **Start time**   :

End time   :

Total Training Time   HRS   MINS

Total Distance Swam

Location ....

Details of the Session

Warm-Up

....
....
....
....

Main Set

....
....
....
....
....

Cool Down

....
....
....

Additional Notes/Information — Coach feedback? Swimming partner details? Areas to work on for next session?

....
....
....

7 SESSION REFLECTION

Date: /   /

Total training time for past 7 sessions: HRS   MINS

Total distance of swimming for past 7 sessions:

Overall, my training sessions for the past 7 days have been:

Excellent   Very Good   Good   Poor

Feedback/Notes From Swim Sessions

....
....
....
....

Other Details   How are you feeling? Is your training progressing as planned? Have you specific goals you wish to achieve for your next 7 training sessions?

....
....
....
....
....
....
....
....
....

"I wouldn't say anything is impossible. I think that everything is possible as long as you put your mind to it and put the time and work into it"

-Michael Phelps-

03
SWIM MEET LOGBOOK

SWIM MEET LOGBOOK

Date: / /   **Start time** :   AM/PM

Location: ....

Age Group: ....

Events Entered:

....
....
....
....

My Performance:

Results: Include times, placings, medals, trophies and awards.

....
....
....
....
....

Coach Feedback:

....
....
....
....

How was your mindset leading up to the swim meet? What can you take from this swim meet to improve for next time? Was their feedback from a coach, friend or someone else that you should record? Do you have a goal for your next swim meet?

....
....
....
....

SWIM MEET LOGBOOK

Date: / /   **Start time** :   AM/PM

Location: ....

Age Group: ....

Events Entered:

....
....
....
....

My Performance:

Results: Include times, placings, medals, trophies and awards.

....
....
....
....
....

Coach Feedback:

....
....
....
....

How was your mindset leading up to the swim meet? What can you take from this swim meet to improve for next time? Was their feedback from a coach, friend or someone else that you should record? Do you have a goal for your next swim meet?

....
....
....
....

SWIM MEET LOGBOOK

Date: / /   **Start time** : AM/PM

Location: ....

Age Group: ....

Events Entered:

....
....
....
....

My Performance:

Results: Include times, placings, medals, trophies and awards.

....
....
....
....
....

Coach Feedback:

....
....
....
....

How was your mindset leading up to the swim meet? What can you take from this swim meet to improve for next time? Was their feedback from a coach, friend or someone else that you should record? Do you have a goal for your next swim meet?

....
....
....
....

SWIM MEET LOGBOOK

Date: / /   **Start time** :   AM/PM

Location: ....

Age Group: ....

Events Entered:

....
....
....
....

My Performance:

Results: Include times, placings, medals, trophies and awards.

....
....
....
....
....

Coach Feedback:

....
....
....
....

How was your mindset leading up to the swim meet? What can you take from this swim meet to improve for next time? Was their feedback from a coach, friend or someone else that you should record? Do you have a goal for your next swim meet?

....
....
....
....

SWIM MEET LOGBOOK

Date: / / **Start time** : AM/PM

Location: ....

Age Group: ....

Events Entered:

....
....
....
....

My Performance:

Results: Include times, placings, medals, trophies and awards.

....
....
....
....
....

Coach Feedback:

....
....
....
....

How was your mindset leading up to the swim meet? What can you take from this swim meet to improve for next time? Was their feedback from a coach, friend or someone else that you should record? Do you have a goal for your next swim meet?

....
....
....
....

SWIM MEET LOGBOOK

Date: / / **Start time** : AM/PM

Location: ....

Age Group: ....

Events Entered:

....
....
....
....

My Performance:

Results: Include times, placings, medals, trophies and awards.

....
....
....
....
....

Coach Feedback:

....
....
....
....

How was your mindset leading up to the swim meet? What can you take from this swim meet to improve for next time? Was their feedback from a coach, friend or someone else that you should record? Do you have a goal for your next swim meet?

....
....
....
....

SWIM MEET LOGBOOK

Date: / /   **Start time** :   AM/PM

Location: ....

Age Group: ....

Events Entered:

....
....
....
....

My Performance:

Results: Include times, placings, medals, trophies and awards.

....
....
....
....
....

Coach Feedback:

....
....
....
....

How was your mindset leading up to the swim meet? What can you take from this swim meet to improve for next time? Was their feedback from a coach, friend or someone else that you should record? Do you have a goal for your next swim meet?

....
....
....
....

SWIM MEET LOGBOOK

Date: / /   **Start time** :   AM/PM

Location: ....

Age Group: ....

Events Entered:

....
....
....
....

My Performance:

Results: Include times, placings, medals, trophies and awards.

....
....
....
....
....

Coach Feedback:

....
....
....
....

How was your mindset leading up to the swim meet? What can you take from this swim meet to improve for next time? Was their feedback from a coach, friend or someone else that you should record? Do you have a goal for your next swim meet?

....
....
....
....

SWIM MEET LOGBOOK

Date: / /   **Start time** :   AM/PM

Location: ....

Age Group: ....

Events Entered:

....
....
....
....

My Performance:

Results: Include times, placings, medals, trophies and awards.

....
....
....
....
....

Coach Feedback:

....
....
....
....

How was your mindset leading up to the swim meet? What can you take from this swim meet to improve for next time? Was their feedback from a coach, friend or someone else that you should record? Do you have a goal for your next swim meet?

....
....
....
....

SWIM MEET LOGBOOK

Date: / / **Start time** : AM/PM

Location: ....

Age Group: ....

Events Entered:

....
....
....
....

My Performance:

Results: Include times, placings, medals, trophies and awards.

....
....
....
....
....

Coach Feedback:

....
....
....
....

How was your mindset leading up to the swim meet? What can you take from this swim meet to improve for next time? Was their feedback from a coach, friend or someone else that you should record? Do you have a goal for your next swim meet?

....
....
....
....

SWIM MEET LOGBOOK

Date: / /   **Start time** :   AM/PM

Location: ....

Age Group: ....

Events Entered:

....
....
....
....

My Performance:

Results: Include times, placings, medals, trophies and awards.

....
....
....
....
....

Coach Feedback:

....
....
....
....

How was your mindset leading up to the swim meet? What can you take from this swim meet to improve for next time? Was their feedback from a coach, friend or someone else that you should record? Do you have a goal for your next swim meet?

....
....
....
....

SWIM MEET LOGBOOK

Date: / / **Start time** : AM/PM

Location: ....

Age Group: ....

Events Entered:

....
....
....
....

My Performance:

Results: Include times, placings, medals, trophies and awards.

....
....
....
....
....

Coach Feedback:

....
....
....
....

How was your mindset leading up to the swim meet? What can you take from this swim meet to improve for next time? Was their feedback from a coach, friend or someone else that you should record? Do you have a goal for your next swim meet?

....
....
....
....

04

Journal Summary, Notes and Favorite Moments

Favorite Moments

Favorite Swim Meet

3 New Swimming Goals

1.
2.
3.

JOURNAL NOTES

JOURNAL NOTES

THE SWIMMERS

Journal

www.ingramcontent.com/pod-product-compliance
Lightning Source LLC
LaVergne TN
LVHW060212080526
838202LV00052B/4259